A Christian Woman's Workbook to Embrace God's Abundance in Your Finances

The *Proverbs 31* Money MINDSET

Michelle W. Fuqua

A Workbook to Help You Transform Your Finances Through Faith Filled Action

The Proverbs 31 Money MINDSET

Michelle W. Fuqua

www.michellewfuqua.com

Follow me on:

@michellewfuqua.com

www.youtube.com/mwfuqua

michelle@michellewfuqua.com

Join the Dream Life Society:
https://tinyurl.com/dreamlifesociety

Join the Ignite Your Purpose Launch Pad:
https://tinyurl.com/igniteyourpurposelaunchpad

Visit My Website at : www.michellewfuqua.com

Get the Self Mastery Guided Journal:
https://BookHip.com/LLSJTP

Hi,

I'm Michelle Fuqua, and mission is to empower high achieving Christian women to uncover their true potential and leave a meaningful legacy.

I am a resilient leader, dedicated pastor, and passionate coach. With a rich background in business, I have spent over 30 years in the energy sector, mastering leadership and mentoring.

As the founding pastor of Living Water Church International, I've been blessed to guide and inspire through faith.

My journey as an author has produced multiple best selling books aimed at helping individuals deepen their relationship with God and find spiritual growth.

I wear multiple hats as a publisher, coach, consultant, and speaker. Based in Atlanta, GA, I strive to reach new heights, impacting lives through my books, group coaching sessions, and engaging talks.

Join me in this journey of faith, resilience, and empowerment, where every challenge is an opportunity to grow and every success a blessing to share.

Michelle W. Fuqua

TABLE OF CONTENTS

MODULE 1

FOUNDATIONS OF AN ABUNDANT MINDSET

LESSON ONE

INTRODUCTION

INTRODUCTION

THE PROVERBS 31 WEALTH BLUEPRINT

How many times have you been in the throes of a financial challenge, while working hard, perhaps making good money, yet not able to make ends meet? Meanwhile, you see others seeming to thrive. Sometimes, we have made poor financial decisions, other times, we just cannot seem to get our ends to meet. Our financial challenges are often caused by our choices, and we need to dig deep to understand our relationship with money. Why do we keep making the same mistakes or end up in the same situations. Why does financial freedom seem to be an elusive dream. This is not how God intends for us to live. Financial freedom is available and achievable when we apply financial practices rooted and grounded in Biblical principles.

Achieving the financial freedom that God promised is not a distant hope when you apply the Biblical principles taught in the Word of God. There are divine promises related to your provisions that apply to your life. These promises when applied to your situations, can produce incredible results.

The goal of this workbook is to walk you through a transformative journey that overlays financial strategies on a foundation of Biblical wisdom. The example of the Proverbs 31 woman provides so many rich insights to this. I like to say that we are developing a Proverbs 31 mindset that involves saving, spending, and sowing. This mindset guides you towards a lifestyle of empowerment and spiritual depth. It is a mindset that yields bold, courageous action.

Over the upcoming lessons, we will look at the profound wisdom of Proverbs 31 to reshape our approach to wealth. You will learn to break through the limitations of scarcity thinking and embrace the mindset of one anchored in God's limitless provisions.

While financial prosperity is the central topic of this workbook, when you align your mindset with God's promises, all areas of your life will benefit. A Godly mindset will lead to a focus on achieving your divine purpose, clarifying your values, making an impact, and leaving a legacy. Your mindset which includes your beliefs, thinking, emotions, and actions determine all your life choices including your finances.

We will examine how viewing money through a Scriptural lens can become an instrument of personal and community gain. You and all those connected to you will benefit! You will have the resources to fulfill God's plan for your life and make a tremendous contribution to building the Kingdom of God.

Let me guide you through these pages on a path to financial freedom and abundance by shining the light on eternal truths related to your resources. Are you ready to uncover and unlock the abundant life promised in the Word of God? Let's go on this journey together, make the necessary adjustments to our mindset and our money, and live out the life already ordained for us!

INTRODUCTION

PROVERBS 31:10-31 (WEB)

Who can find a worthy woman?
For her price is far above rubies.

The heart of her husband trusts in her.
He shall have no lack of gain.

She does him good, and not harm,
all the days of her life.

She seeks wool and flax,
and works eagerly with her hands.

She is like the merchant ships.
She brings her bread from afar.

She rises also while it is yet night,
gives food to her household,
and portions for her servant girls.

She considers a field, and buys it.
With the fruit of her hands, she plants a vineyard.

She arms her waist with strength,
and makes her arms strong.

She perceives that her merchandise is profitable. Her lamp doesn't go out by night. Her lamp doesn't go out by night.

She lays her hands to the distaff,
and her hands hold the spindle.

She opens her arms to the poor;
yes, she extends her hands to the needy.

She is not afraid of the snow for her household; for all her household are clothed with scarlet.

She makes for herself carpets of tapestry.
Her clothing is fine linen and purple.

Her husband is respected in the gates,
when he sits among the elders of the land.

She makes linen garments and sells them,
and delivers sashes to the merchant.

Strength and dignity are her clothing. She laughs at the time to come.

She opens her mouth with wisdom.
Kind instruction is on her tongue.

She looks well to the ways of her household, and doesn't eat the bread of idleness.

Her children rise up and call her blessed.
Her husband also praises her:

"Many women do noble things, but you excel them all."

Charm is deceitful, and beauty is vain;
but a woman who fears Yahweh, she shall be praised.

Give her of the fruit of her hands! Let her works praise her in the gates!

INTRODUCTION

PRINCIPLES FROM THE PROVERBS 31 WOMAN

Your Value and Self-Worth is PRICELESS
Proverbs 31:10 - "Who can find a worthy woman? For her price is far above rubies."

You are a rare jewel of finding. There is no one else like you. Setting a value to you would be a disservice because all the money and riches in the world cannot come close to your value.

There are certain rubies that are so rare that their value is higher than diamonds. While our modern society holds the diamond as high value, you as a virtuous woman are priceless and rare. You are worthy of the abundance that comes through your obedience to God.

You are Trustworthy and Reliable
Proverbs 31:11 - "The heart of her husband trusts in her, and he shall have no lack of gain."

Trustworthiness is as a key trait. In any role – be it personal, professional, or spiritual – cultivating trust and demonstrating reliability allow you to develop core relationships and life habits that yield success. Consistency, dependability, and integrity are a dynamic trio.

You are Willing to do the Work!
Proverbs 31:13 - "She seeks wool and flax, and works eagerly with her hands."

The account of the woman seeking wool and flax and working eagerly underscores the principle of diligence. She goes in search of her success and there is an implication in her actions. She does not expect to be defeated by hardship and obstacles. She expects to receive reward from her efforts. Success requires a strong work ethic, commitment to tasks, and the willingness to put in the necessary effort.

INTRODUCTION

PRINCIPLES FROM THE PROVERBS 31 WOMAN

You Have an Entrepreneurial Spirit
Proverbs 31:16 - "She considers a field, and buys it. With the fruit of her hands, she plants a vineyard."

The entrepreneurial spirit is powerful! She considers what is before her and makes sound financial decisions. See yourself in her.

Your financial understanding grows as you execute on your purpose activities. You consider a field and buy it, and perceive that her merchandise is profitable. This reflects entrepreneurial spirit and financial wisdom. Being savvy in business, managing resources effectively, and making informed decisions are key skills for success.

You are a Giver
Proverbs 31:20 - "She opens her arms to the poor; yes, she extends her hands to the needy."

Our lady demonstrates community engagement and philanthropy. She is generous to those in need. True leadership and personal growth involve not just personal success, but also giving back to the community and helping those in need.

You Have a Plan and Prepare to Execute It
Proverbs 31:21 - "She is not afraid of the snow for her household; for all her household are clothed with scarlet."

Preparation for the seasons of life ensures that you have what you need. She is equipped to meet the winter and no one in her home is without a coat. They are richly dressed in scarlet. This does not happen by accident. She has put in the time to plan and prepare for the winter.

You Communicate with Wisdom and Grace
Proverbs 31:26 - "She opens her mouth with wisdom; and in her tongue is the law of kindness."

What we speak will rule our lives. Speak with wisdom and kindness. A soft tone, and empathy will carry you far. Speak with wisdom based on what you know and not what you see. Share knowledge and advice in a way that uplifts and educates others.

INTRODUCTION

PRINCIPLES FROM THE PROVERBS 31 WOMAN

You Have an Entrepreneurial Spirit
Proverbs 31:16 - "She considers a field, and buys it. With the fruit of her hands, she plants a vineyard."

The entrepreneurial spirit in this lady is powerful! She considers what is before her and makes sound financial decisions.

Your financial understanding grows as you execute on your purpose activities. You consider a field and buy it, and perceive that your merchandise is profitable. This reflects an entrepreneurial spirit and financial wisdom. Being savvy in business, managing resources effectively, and making informed decisions are key skills for success.

You are a Giver
Proverbs 31:20 - "She opens her arms to the poor; yes, she extends her hands to the needy."

This lady demonstrates community engagement and philanthropy. She is generous to those in need. True leadership and personal growth involve personal success, giving back to the community, and helping those in need.

You Have a Plan and Prepare to Execute It
Proverbs 31:21 - "She is not afraid of the snow for her household; for all her household are clothed with scarlet."

This lady is prepared for the seasons of life. She is equipped to meet the winter and no one in her home is without a coat. They are richly dressed in scarlet. This does not happen by accident. She has put in the time to plan and prepare for the winter.

You Communicate with Wisdom and Grace
Proverbs 31:26 - "She opens her mouth with wisdom; and in her tongue is the law of kindness."

What we speak will rule our lives. Our lady speaks with wisdom and kindness. A soft tone, and empathy will carry you far. Speak with wisdom based on what you know and not what you see. Share knowledge and advice in a way that uplifts and educates others.

LESSON TWO

THE POWER OF A PROVERBS 31 MINDSET

By trusting God's promise of provision, we empower ourselves to achieve financial freedom. We are blessed to be a blessing!

EMBRACING FAITH-DRIVEN ABUNDANCE FOR FINANCIAL EMPOWERMENT

Faith will transform your approach to your finances. Adopting a Proverbs 31 mindset (P31M) gives you divine inspiration, unlocks your God-given potential, and releases the fullness of God's blessings. When you understand and embrace the P31M, your financial journey will be transformed, sometimes slowly, sometimes overtime, but you will move from a distant dream to possibility to reality. P31M empowers you to approach financial decisions with Godly confidence, seize opportunities with faith, and create a life of both material and spiritual abundance.

The virtuous woman described in Proverbs 31 allows us to develop a model for a successful life, mindset and work ethic. Her mindset demonstrates the power of faith in building financial success. The P31M encourages a courageous, productive, and optimistic approach to wealth that is guided by Scriptural wisdom. The P31M rejects a focus on scarcity, limiting beliefs, and fear. Negativity is replaced with faith in God's promises, obedience to His instructions, and strategic work and rest. Note that the old way of thinking was holding you back from achieving your dreams in every area of life. But we are talking about money right now! The fear attached to that old way of thinking paralyzes you and prevents you from taking advantage of opportunities. Also, that perspective leads to avoiding necessary risks thereby missing out on the blessings of God that have your name on them.

THE POWER OF A PROVERBS 31 MINDSET

Proverbs 31 inspires us to see beyond our limitations and trust in God's abundance. When I read about this woman, I am encouraged and motivated to shine! I am ready to do the work! She is a boss, and she demonstrates her mindset through her actions. Cultivating a mindset of Biblical abundance involves nurturing the spiritual disciplines of thanksgiving and gratitude, affirmation of God's promises, visualizing faith driven success, documenting the vision, and building our circle of like minded souls who are on the same path.

While financial prosperity is a result, and can also be a valid intention, the results lead to spiritual growth. Peace, joy, and community are a few of the many benefits. Let's go ahead and settle the issue that holds so many of us back. God is okay with us reaping a financial harvest when we work, serve, and make the world a better place! You do not have to be poor to be a good Christian. Being rich does not make you a good Christian either. It is not about the money; it is about your attitude.

The P31M is exemplified in the actions and qualities of the Proverbs 31 woman, an example of Biblical wisdom, strength, and diligence. She demonstrates the ability to effectively blend her spirituality with her practicality, especially in her family business. Her management of land and goods reveals wisdom, enterprise, and strategy. She trusts God to provide and does not yield to fear and scarcity.

Her confidence in God's goodness motivates her behavior. Her family is her treasure, and she knows how to work for what they need. She willingly works with her hands ensuring her financial needs are met. She is thoughtful about what she buys. She is generous, and ready to meet the demands of those in need.

She demonstrates her work ethic by her eagerness to work with her hands to provide for her household. She takes what she earns and multiplies it through smart business moves. She does not spend all of it, and she does not bury it in a hole where it will not grow. She obviously has discernment, strategic planning, and courage to make financial decisions that probably involves risk and reward. She is recognized in her community as a businesswoman, wife, and mother. She is God assured and gives us a model to live by. By emulating her, you can take an all-inclusive faith-based approach to your financial stewardship. The foundation for your financial stewardship should be based on faith, wisdom, hard work, and charitable giving.

PROVERBS 31 MINDSET SHIFTS

From Scarcity to Resourcefulness: Instead of focusing on what she lacks, the Proverbs 31 woman teaches us to be resourceful with what we have. She demonstrates that abundance is not just about having more, but about using what you have effectively and creatively, as seen in her ability to create and manage her resources wisely (v. 13, 16).

From Solely Receiving to Generously Giving: Moving from a mindset of merely receiving to one of generously giving is a key shift. The Proverbs 31 woman extends her hand to the poor and needy (v. 20), showing that abundance involves not just personal gain, but also the ability to give back and support others.

From Fear to Faith: Rather than fearing the future, the Proverbs 31 woman faces it from a place of faith with strength and dignity (v. 25). This reflects a mindset of confidence and optimism, believing in the abundance of future opportunities and being prepared to embrace them.

From Passivity to Proactive Engagement: The P31 woman is actively engaged in her life and work, not waiting for opportunities but creating them. This proactive approach to life (v. 18, 24) is a key aspect of an abundance mindset, where action and initiative lead to growth and success.

From Singular Focus to Diverse Interests: The diverse activities and skills of the Proverbs 31 woman (from managing a household to engaging in trade) suggest an abundance mindset is not limited to one area of expertise or interest. Embracing a variety of skills and pursuits can lead to a more abundant life.

From Self-Doubt to Confidence: Embracing your worth and abilities is crucial. The Proverbs 31 woman is valued "far above rubies" (v. 10), indicating the importance of recognizing and believing in one's intrinsic value, which is key to an abundance mindset.

From Isolation to Community Engagement: The Proverbs 31 woman is not isolated; she is actively engaged in her community. She contributes to the well being of her household and society (v. 20, 23). Understanding that abundance flows through relationships and community involvement is essential.

THE POWER OF A PROVERBS 31 MINDSET

Take a moment to consider your current beliefs about money and wealth. Jot down what first comes to mind. Then, consider the principles demonstrated by the Proverbs 31 woman and other teachings on abundance. How do your beliefs align? Consider also what you learned as a child from watching or hearing your parents or other influences in your life. Why do you think you believe what you believe about money? Finally, what might Scripture say to reshape your perspective on money and wealth?

Explain how your money mindset affects your current and or future financial decision and or actions, in what way would that change if your view shifted to a provocative 31 woman, faith-based life of unlimited abundance?

THE POWER OF A PROVERBS 31 MINDSET

Is there someone you know in your sphere of influence (in your community or the Bible) who demonstrates a strong P31 mindset in their financial life? What qualities and/or behaviors do they exhibit that align with the principles of Proverbs 31? What about these principles would you like to incorporate into your own financial life?

Identify three financial objectives you want to meet within the next year. How will adopting an abundance mindset contribute to your staying driven and focused on reaching these goals?

1.

2.

3.

THE POWER OF A PROVERBS 31 MINDSET

Journal about what you thought of the first time you realized that you needed to grow your wealth from the current level. How did you feel? Were you upset? What could you have done to approach the situation in a different way? Or, think of a time when the abundant availability of money caused you to make poor decisions?

THE POWER OF A PROVERBS 31 MINDSET

Envision how your financial situation will be dramatically different five years from now, once you shift your mindset and behaviors. Describe how this might look and feel in your future day to day life. Describe in vivid detail.

THE POWER OF A PROVERBS 31 MINDSET

Close your eyes and visualize yourself really taking in the whole idea of living abundantly and not having to barely get by. Or just having enough for necessities. What financial choices would you make differently? What opportunities would you be in pursuit of?

Think about your financial life and write three things you are grateful for when it comes to money and finances.

1.

2.

3.

IDENTIFYING AND OVERCOMING SCARCITY THINKING

Jen received a large lump sum bonus that represents more than the average person makes annually. Her stomach hurt and her stress level skyrocketed. She pondered to herself, "What should I do with the money?" Even though she had plenty, she warred with fear of losing the money. Instead of viewing the windfall as a blessing, it became a curse. The more she made, the less settled she became. Her actuality began to align with this scarcity-based fear because her actions were not in alignment with growth.

On the other hand, Patrice received the same bonus. She saw the payments as an opportunity to expand her financial footprint. She had a constructive plan, and she was not afraid to execute it. She was also not afraid of losing the money. She experienced excitement and gratitude for what she received. Her actions demonstrated her belief and she took bold actions to multiply her resources.

These ladies demonstrated the two schools of thought at play in this situation. Scarcity thinking and faith thinking. One leads to shrinkage while the other leads to abundance. What is your thinking like? Have you ever, or do you now have a problem with a scarcity mindset? How you answer the following questions will give you a gauge to determine your current thinking temperament. Do you focus on lack and limitation? Adjusting your thoughts and beliefs is the way to overcome this mindset. It is also tied to your self esteem. Do you believe that you deserve what you have? Another clue is fear related to your security and well being.

Do you emphasize what is lacking so much so that it overshadows the blessings and opportunities provided by God? You may have money in the bank, but you are still afraid of going broke. This is not how God would have us to think, and the resulting actions sabotage our ability to get wealth. Overcoming this way of thinking facilitates the flow of the many blessing that God releases into our lives.

Spend time reflecting about your thinking. How does your thoughts and mindset agree or disagree with the promises of God? How do your actions align with the principles demonstrated by the Proverbs 31 woman. Do you worry excessively about finances? Are you reluctant to invest in basic necessities? Do you feel envy when others are blessed or appear to have more than you? What about a gnawing, pervasive feeling of insufficiency?

The P31M finds a way to see the abundance in the midst of not having enough today. The deficiency motivates the P31M to get moving with what God has shown you. The P31M woman is glad to see others prosper and looks for ways to help them along the way. The antidote for scarcity thinking is Biblically based abundance thinking. Grab hold of the truth of God's Word concerning your money and train your brain to believe it, receive it, and achieve it.

Some practical actions we can take to do this include reflecting on what we have as opposed to what we lack. Express gratitude for the abundance that you find when you shift your mindset. Gratitude is a great way to transform your attitude and your thoughts. You learn to appreciate your current situation as well as your ability to make positive movement towards the abundance you desire.

Some practical actions we can take to do this include reflecting on what we have as opposed to what we lack. Express gratitude for the abundance that you find when you shift your mindset. Gratitude is a great way to transform your attitude and your thoughts. You learn to appreciate your current situation as well as your ability to make positive movement towards the abundance you desire.

For many years, my pastors and other Christian teachers expressed the importance of my mind, thinking and thoughts. Today, I am challenging you to challenge your thinking. If the thought does not agree with the promise, then the thought has to be rejected as a lie and replaced with truth. Make the thought true based on God's Word!

How did we end up with these faulty mindsets? You should spend time thinking about your money story and how you started down the mindset path that you are on. Study the Word to heal your mind and attitude. Pray and ask God to help you to trust Him with your finances so that you can make bold, aligned money management moves. Write out truth statements geared towards deleting old negative thought patterns. Think about faith and hope, and trust in God's plans for your financial well-being.

Take the time to create a financial plan with clear goals in the presence of God. This means to pray over it, and move with intention and faith. This will give you clarity of direction, confidence in your path, and freedom from money related anxiety.

By cultivating a P31M inspired mindset, grounded in faith and empowerment, you open the doors to divine prosperity, security, and fulfillment in your financial life.

IDENTIFYING AND OVERCOMING SCARCITY THINKING

Which life event or person has influenced your mindset towards a limited supply instead of abundance?

In what areas of your life do you know and experience a sense of more-than-enough-ness or abundance, and how can you learn from and apply this mindset to your financial life?

IDENTIFYING AND OVERCOMING SCARCITY THINKING

Could your thoughts and ideas about money be holding you back from financial success? What are some of these common money myths. Could one of these be holding you back from your prosperity and abundance?

What would your life look like if you achieved financial abundance, and what are some steps that you could take daily in order to bring your vision closer to reality?

CULTIVATING POSITIVE BELIEFS & ATTITUDES TOWARDS MONEY

Self-Reflection

Take a few moments to contemplate your present attitudes and beliefs toward money. Look deeply at each negative opinion, limiting belief, or feelings you have about money. Really dig deep to focus on where these negative ideas originated.

Challenge Negative Beliefs

See if you have any misconceptions about money that are going to get in your way. Are they true, or did somebody tell you that they were and you believed them?

Positive Affirmations

Create positive affirmations that you relate to and can say everyday. A perfect example is "I attract wealth and abundance." Affirmations need to be individual to you!

Financial Education

Learn about personal finance. Get to know the ins and outs of how to budget your money, how to invest and make money, and the different ways that you can make money in the world.

Surround Yourself with Positivity

Build a tribe of supportive people who have a healthy outlook and mindset and are pursuing their dreams in life.

Stay Committed

Don't give up on your vision. Be committed to the process. Take the necessary, daily steps on your journey. Enjoy each day.

CULTIVATING POSITIVE BELIEFS & ATTITUDES TOWARDS MONEY

List three positive or happy experiences you have about money. How can you use these positive memories to reframe your view of money to one that is constructive in building your financial dreams?

1.

2.

3.

What are the negative beliefs or attitudes you have related to money. Re-frame these thoughts with Scripture based beliefs that empower you and support your financial goals?

CULTIVATING POSITIVE BELIEFS & ATTITUDES TOWARDS MONEY

What are your current financial accomplishments? Count everything, regardless of magnitude. Can leaning into these successes encourage you to manage your money effectively?

Consider the role of money in your life goals and values. How can you ensure that your spending habits are in accordance to your values and are creating the sense of meaning and fulfillment that you want?

CHALLENGE YOUR IMPOSSIBLE

WITH GOD

ALL THINGS ARE

POSSIBLE

LESSON THREE

BUILD A SOLID, BIBLICAL FOUNDATION

STEWARDSHIP AND PLANNING: LESSONS FROM THE PROVERBS 31 WOMAN

She looks well to the ways of her household and eats not the bread of idleness.
Proverbs 31:27

Stewardship is the art of purposeful planning leading to sustainable success.
In other words, she is a good steward. Wikipedia has a great definition of stewardship: "An ethical value that embodies the responsible planning and management of resources. The Christian version would add that God entrusts the resources to us. God gives money to us and strengthens our hands to get money. We should infuse gratitude in everything we do, and not take for granted when we have the resources to purchase small or large items. Budgeting and managing your finances are practical acts that exemplify the P31 mindset. Tracking income and expenses allow us to have a clear picture of the allocation of our financial resources.

We can see areas of overspending and then change our spending to align with our priorities. Essential needs should never suffer because of non-essential spending. Overspending can lead us to live outside of our means through growing debt liabilities. Proverbs 22:7 reminds us that the borrower is a servant to the lender. We are called to be the lenders and NOT the borrowers. Building a God only knows (GOK) fund (Pastor Charles H. Jackson, Sr.) better known as an emergency stash, will also mitigate needing to use debt to cover your expenses. Take debt management seriously. By managing and reviving your budget, spending, and debt, you create flexibility and agility. When life throws you a curb ball, you are prepared to respond. The overall well-being of your family will benefit when you execute a spiritually infused financial plan.

7 KEY STEPS FOR CREATING A BUDGETING AND FINANCIAL PLAN

1. Assess Your Current Financial Situation

Calculate income, track expenses, and identify areas to cut back for better financial management.

2. Set Financial Goals

Set SMART financial goals by determining short-term (within a year), medium-term (1-5 years), and long-term (5 years or more) objectives that are specific, measurable, achievable, relevant, and time-bound for effective progress tracking.

3. Create and Track Your Budget

Effectively manage your income by dividing it into categories, prioritizing essentials, setting aside savings and investments, and budgeting for discretionary spending. Use budgeting tools and regularly review your expenses and progress against the budget to manage your finances effectively.

4. Build an Emergency Fund

Save for emergencies: Create an emergency fund with at least 3-6 months' worth of living expenses to cover unexpected situations.

5. Prioritise Debt Repayment

Allocate extra funds towards paying off high-interest debts to reduce financial stress and free up more money for savings and investments.

6. Invest for the Future

Discover diverse investment options like stocks, bonds, mutual funds, and real estate to grow your wealth, and consult a financial adviser for personalised guidance aligned with your risk tolerance and financial objectives.

7. Review and Adjust Regularly

Regularly review and adjust your budget and financial plan to accommodate changes in income, expenses, and life circumstances, ensuring progress towards your goals.

Staying proactive and mindful of your financial choices will help you build a strong foundation for financial security and success.

BUILDING AN EMERGENCY FUND: A REFLECTION OF FAITH

She is not afraid of the snow.... Proverbs 31:21

Putting aside funds for those unexpected life events will save you from unnecessary worry. There are a few good reasons to do this:

- Ride through seasons of low to no employment.
- Lessen the impact of medical emergencies.
- Pay for major household repairs
- Any other unexpected expenses

In the Proverb about the ant, he works all summer packing away food so that he has enough to make it through the winter (Proverbs 6:6-11). Your fund is supported by Biblical principles of planning and preparedness. There are some who would say that having an emergency fund is not an act of faith. The Bible is replete with principles and wisdom pertaining to preparing. Preparation is an act of stewardship and the Proverbs 31 woman had barns and fields. She had plenty of things she could sell if she had a need. What do you have that you can use to meet any emergencies?

Do not beat yourself up if the answer is, "not enough!" Build a strategy and start saving today. Start small based on what you have available. Financial advisors recommend saving three to six months' worth of living expenses. An emergency fund is a wall of protection or buffer that holds off calamity when it comes. Jesus said that we would have trouble and tribulations, but He has already overcome it all (John 16:33). We agree with our victory already in process by building our nest egg. That nest egg is also your barrier against debt. When we do not have cash flow, we will often use debt to get through the rough spells. Before we know it, we are in debt. Debt works like investments but in a negative way. We become the investment for the bank and they get rich off of all the interest we pay them. That interest payment can eat into our available cash flow making it impossible for us to concentrate on our life and financial goals. Go ahead and make up your mind that you will implement this fund as soon as possible. Start small and increase your regular amount over time.

ESTABLISHING AN EMERGENCY FUND FOR SECURITY AND PEACE OF MIND

Why is it important for you to have an emergency fund? What are some burdens that this fund could relieve? How would you feel if you had several months of savings?

Set a goal for your emergency fund. Will you save a certain number of months of income, or a set amount? By what date? Write down your plan for achieving this goal.

ESTABLISHING AN EMERGENCY FUND FOR SECURITY AND PEACE OF MIND

Based on your current spending habits and budget, where can you make adjustments so you can build your emergency fund? Identify areas where you can cut back on expenses to increase your savings.

Visualise the feeling of having a fully-funded emergency fund. Describe how it would positively impact your daily life and alleviate stress during uncertain times.

MANAGING DEBT AND USING CREDIT WISELY

The borrower is servant to the lender. Proverbs 22:7-9

Managing debt and credit wisely are crucial to responsible stewardship. Prioritize the payment of high-interest debts can relieve your financial burden quicker. It's essential to reduce the accumulation of excessive interest.

Creating a budget that includes debt repayments alongside living expenses can help you stay disciplined. Discipline will prevent unnecessary spending and racking up new debt. To do this, learn to live within your means. Don't spend it if you do not have it to spend. We should refrain from making debt our safety cushion. Pay your debt on time to protect and build your credit score. Your financial integrity is an important part of your Christian witness. This practice enhances your financial credibility. In those times when you decide to use debt for certain purchases or in your business, a good credit score will make borrowing money less expensive.

When it comes to using credit cards, be responsible. Avoid excessive spending on credit. Reduce accumulation of high interest balances by paying in full each month. I am sure that the Proverbs 31 woman used leverage when necessary in her business dealings. Her financial integrity and hard work were her credit score. Some equate a frugal lifestyle with stinginess. There is a balance and you will need to find the balance that works for you. Consider saving for major purchases instead of using credit as an automatic solution. When you live by your budget, reduce the use of credit, and plan for your spending, you strengthen your financial foundation. These principles are rooted in biblical teachings, and pave the way for long-term financial success.

MANAGING DEBT AND USING CREDIT WISELY

Add up your debt. How much debt do you have, and what types of debts (credit cards, loans, etc.) do you owe? Write down your feelings and emotions about your debt to gain clarity on your financial situation.

What financial goals could you achieve if you were able to reduce or eliminate your debts? Describe how being debt-free would impact your life positively.

MANAGING DEBT AND USING CREDIT WISELY

Explore your spending habits and patterns related to credit card usage. Do you tend to use credit cards for unnecessary purchases or impulse buys? How can you develop better spending habits and use credit cards more responsibly?

List your debts in order of priority, and determine how much money you can allocate each month towards paying them off. Write about the progress you make as you work towards becoming debt-free.

MANAGING DEBT AND USING CREDIT WISELY

MODULE 2

PRACTICAL MONEY MANAGEMENT AND INVESTMENT STRATEGIES

LESSON FOUR

BUILDING SMART MONEY PROVERBS 31 HABITS

DEVELOPING EFFECTIVE MONEY MANAGEMENT SKILLS

Embracing Budgeting as a Spiritual Discipline

Knowing how to manage your money is the key to controlling your finances so that you can achieve your financial goals. We must adapt strategies and habits, grounded in Christian principles, that allow us to handle income, expenses, and investments. Making informed financial decisions will help you to gain confidence in your abilities. You will see the fruit of your decisions as your situation changes. If you did not learn how to manage your money from your parents, school, or some other qualified professional, you can still learn. Do not be afraid to seek help from professionals who are experienced at managing money.

Attend workshops and free training in your area or virtual. Become a student of your finances. Learn how money works so that you can cause it to multiply. When God gives it to you, He expects you to make it multiply. Learn how money works so that you can cause it to multiply. When God gives it to you, He expects you to make it multiply.

DEVELOPING EFFECTIVE MONEY MANAGEMENT SKILLS

Saving is an Act of Trust

Saving is the foundation of implementing your money management system. As we have discussed in previous sections, saving is in agreement with wise planning and stewardship. It is in alignment with trusting God with your finances. Saving regularly builds the habit of saving for emergencies and for future projects, goals, and giving. I cannot over stress that setting aside a portion of your income for savings is an act of faith.

Budgeting is a Spiritual Discipline

I teach a lot about spiritual disciplines of prayer, study, meditation, and fasting. What if we approached financial stewardship as if it were a spiritual discipline. Spiritual disciplines are powerful because they connect us to the Holy Spirit and build our natural resilience—"bouncebackability." If we approach our finances as if they were (because they are) spiritual disciplines, we would be inviting the Holy Spirit to lead, guide and direct our money. We cannot out produce God. If we cooperate with Him for our money, our financial world will be transformed astronomically. A Holy Spirit directed budget can serve as a clear roadmap for financial decisionmaking. This will lead to effective prioritization so that our essential needs are met, and savings and investments are implemented. The Proverbs 31 woman shows us how to achieve this through the way she managed her home and business.

DEVELOPING EFFECTIVE MONEY MANAGEMENT SKILLS

Practice Mindful Spending: A Biblical Perspective

Intentionality in our spending involves evaluating needs versus wants. It is essential that we make informed choices to avoid impulsive purchases and unnecessary expenses. Pray before you do your plan and listen for His leading. You will develop wise discernment that will help you to achieve your financial goals.

Regular Review and Adaptation: Staying on Course

Review your financial progress regularly and adjust your strategies as needed. This attention is key to effective money management. Stay proactive and adaptable, with an eye on both current needs and future goals. This keeps you on track towards your financial objectives. It also reflects the Biblical principle of diligent stewardship and continuous growth.

Conclusion

Take charge of your financial future by developing these money management skills, grounded in Scriptural wisdom. Remember that you are not in this alone, God is working in you, with you, and through you. There are professionals who will help you also. Using all of these approaches reduces financial stress and aligns your financial practices with your faith, leading towards long term prosperity and peace of mind. Your long term peace of mind and prosperity is the fruit of your labor.

DEVELOPING EFFECTIVE MONEY MANAGEMENT SKILLS

What is your current financial situation, and where do you see areas for improvement?

What are your short-term, medium-term, and long-term financial goals, and why are they important to you?

How can you create a budget that aligns with your financial objectives and what challenges might you face in the process?

What saving and investment strategies will you explore, considering risks and potential rewards?

How will you track your progress, reflect on your financial habits, and learn from challenges along the way?

TRACKING EXPENSES AND SETTING FINANCIAL GOALS

Tracking your expenses and setting financial goals are two key foundations of effective money management. Keeping a close eye on income and expenditures, and setting clear financial goals let you take control of your finances and your future.

To track expenses, keep up with your money's sources and expenditures. Understanding where the money is going helps you to become more aware of ways to save money, as well as how to make wise financials choices.

One of the key components of successful money management is having clear financial goals. Financial goals give you something to work toward and help you feel a sense of purpose with your money. They can help you make wise spending decisions and focus your saving and investing efforts.

People who set financial goals must pay attention to those goals and evaluate consistently how they are doing. Staying connected to your plans increases your chances of achieving them. Financial goals fall into three categories. They are short-term goals, medium-term goals, and long-term goals.

Financial goals should also be SMART. SMART is the acronym for: specific, measurable, attainable, realistic, and time-bound. SMART financial goals are goals that are Specific, Measurable, Assignable, Realistic, and Time-limited.

If you are really serious about putting together a realistic budget that satisfies your aspirations, combine expense tracking (don't worry, we will get to this) with goal setting, which we talk about next! By tracking progress towards goals it is easier to keep motivated and capable in the money game!

Reevaluation of routine and expected expenditure is essential to an optimal use of money. Life circumstances change, needs evolve over time and setting new targets, and this calls for proper adjustments to keep up with the pace of a secure financial future.

TRACKING EXPENSES AND SETTING FINANCIAL GOALS

Take a week to track all your expenses, no matter how small. How does this exercise make you feel, and what patterns or surprises do you notice about your spending habits?

Reflect on your short-term and long-term financial goals. Which goals are the most important to you, and how can aligning your spending with these priorities help you achieve them faster?

Develop a budget that encompasses your income, fixed expenses, and discretionary spending. What steps can you take to ensure that your budget is both effective and flexible enough to accommodate unexpected expenses?

Review your tracked expenses. Are there any areas where you tend to overspend or could potentially cut back? Write about strategies you can implement to curb unnecessary spending.

USING THE SMART FRAMEWORK FOR FINANCIAL GOALS

Specific

Clearly define what you want to achieve with your finances. For instance, "Save $10,000 for an emergency fund," or "Pay off $5,000 of credit card debt this year." Your goals should be direct and clear, reflecting a focused intention.

Measurable

Ensure that your goals are quantifiable. For example, instead of saying "save more money," specify an amount and timeline, like "save $200 per month."

Achievable

Your goals should be realistic and attainable. Consider your current financial situation and resources. Pray for guidance and wisdom to set goals that are challenging yet possible with God's help.

Relevant

Align your goals with your broader financial plan and Christian values. For example, setting a goal to save for a family vacation, retirement, or tithing aligns with both your financial health and spiritual life.

Action Steps

Write Down Your Goals:

- Documenting your goals solidifies them and serves as a constant reminder. Keep them in a place where you will see them regularly, like a journal, a financial planner, or a digital document.

Plan Your Steps:

- Break down your goals into smaller, actionable steps. If your goal is to save $10,000 in a year, determine how much you need to save each month, then identify specific areas in your budget to cut back or ways to increase your income.

Regular Review and Prayer:

- Regularly review your progress towards your goals. Pray for guidance, strength, and discipline to stay on track. Adjust your plans as needed, always aligning your financial actions with biblical wisdom and your faith journey.

Seek Accountability:

- Share your goals with a trusted friend, family member, or financial advisor who can offer support, advice, and accountability.

The SMART goal-setting framework can be effectively utilized to define and achieve your financial objectives in a way that harmonizes with Christian teachings and the wisdom of the Proverbs 31 woman.

S

Specific Goals:

____

____

____

____

M

Measurable Goals:

____

____

____

____

A

Achievable Goals:

____

____

____

____

R

Relevant Goals:

____

____

____

____

T

Time-Bound Goals:

____

____

____

____

GUIDE TO SAVING AND INVESTING FOR THE FUTURE

Start Early

Begin saving and investing as soon as possible to take advantage of the power of compounding and give your money more time to grow.

Assess Financial Situation

Evaluate your current financial situation and understand your risk tolerance and financial objectives.

Create a Budget

Develop a budget that allows you to set aside a portion of your income and prioritise essential expenses, allocate funds for goals.

Build an Emergency Fund

This safety net protects you from unexpected financial setbacks.

Establish Short-Term Goals

Define short-term financial goals and allocate funds towards these goals in your budget.

Contribute Regularly

Be consistent in your savings and investment contributions, even small amounts contribute to significant growth over time.

Monitor and Adjust

Regularly review your finances and assess its performance against your financial goals, make adjustments as needed to stay on track.

Stay Disciplined

Remain committed to your saving and investing plan, avoid emotional decision-making and focus on your long-term objectives.

OUR LIVES FLOURISH WHEN WE EMBRACE THE PATH OF GROWTH

LESSON FIVE

DIVERSIFYING WEALTH: THE PROVERBS 31 ACCUMULATION STRATEGY

EXPLORING VARIOUS INCOME STREAMS AND OPPORTUNITIES

When exploring income generating ideas, focus on the right decision for your finances, especially how long you can afford to be in an investment. Some investments work for others based on their cash flow and savings but may not work for you. Focus on your financial outlook. You also need to understand your risk tolerance. Can you watch your investment fluctuate in real time or do you need something more stable. There is a correlation between risk and reward; find the right blend for your temperament and bank account.

By all means, pray about it, and ask God for discernment, to guide you in choosing a few things that could make you money and fit into your life. The Proverbs 31 woman is a model of balance. Her story reflects a woman committed to handling her business every day. I imagine her motivation is her family. What is your motivation? What is your why? Knowing these answers help you to stay the course and make good money decisions.

The Proverbs 31 woman is a living example of the power of continuous growth and strategic planning. She looks at all the ways she can make money and applies wisdom and knowledge to her decisions, creating new income streams as a result. Like her, keep up with market trends, network with a purpose, and volunteer according to your passion. Your current efforts either produce tomorrow's overflow or today's drought. The strategy of diversifying your income needs to be taken with caution, not greed. See it as a chance to ignite the potential that is simmering inside you and to open doors of opportunity that are already waiting on you. Income streams lead to a strong and solid financial foundation. This diversification makes every financial journey align with a meaningful and purposeful life. Your expanding life will, in turn, expand your wallet.

IDEAS FOR DIFFERENT TYPES OF PASSIVE INCOME STREAMS

Royalties from Creative Work

You can earn royalties from your creative work, such as books, art, music, videos, or images.

Dividend Investing

Invest in dividend stocks or funds. You earn regular dividends without actively managing the investments.

Digital Products

Create and sell digital products, such as e-books, online courses, software, or photography presets.

Rental Income

Purchase property (real estate) and rent it out to tenants. This can be residential or commercial property.

Affiliate Marketing

Promote products or services through affiliate links and earn a commission through your referrals.

Automated Online Businesses

Build and run automated online businesses, such as dropshipping stores or print-on-demand.

High-Yield Savings Accounts or CDs

Park your money in high-yield savings accounts or certificates of deposit (CDs) to earn interest.

Real Estate Crowdfunding

Invest in real estate projects through crowdfunding platforms, where you can pool funds with other investors.

License Your Ideas or Inventions

If you have unique inventions or ideas, license them to companies and earn royalties.

Peer-to-Peer Lending

There are platforms where you lend money to individuals or businesses and earn interest on the loans.

Rental Properties for Vehicles / Equipment

Rent out vehicles, equipment, or tools that you own for passive income.

Peer-to-Peer Lending or Crowdfunding

Generate income by lending money through peer-to-peer lending platforms or investing in crowdfunding projects that offer returns.

EXPLORING VARIOUS INCOME STREAMS AND OPPORTUNITIES

What are your unique skills, talents, and passions? How can you leverage them to identify potential income streams or business opportunities?

Investigate different income streams and opportunities that align with your interests. What are the pros and cons of each option, and how might they fit into your long-term financial goals?

Take some time to brainstorm creative income-generating ideas that haven't been explored yet. Write down any wild or innovative concepts that come to mind.

For each potential income stream, research the market demand and competition. Are there untapped niches or areas with high demand that you could explore?

Which income streams align best with your objectives, and how can you prioritise your efforts to achieve them?

DIVERSIFYING INVESTMENTS FOR LONG-TERM GROWTH

The wisdom of the Proverbs 31 woman to steward her resources also applies in the basic principle of diversification as an investment strategy. The goal of diversification is to minimize the risk in your portfolio by spreading your investments among various asset classes and sectors so that even if a particular security or asset class does poorly the other assets will hopefully make up for those losses.

Ecclesiastics 11:1-2 gives us a clue to the mindset of the wisest man in history, Solomon, "Cast your bread on the waters; for you shall find it after many days. Give a portion to seven, yes, even to eight; for you don't know what evil will be on the earth." We can spend considerable time figuring out what Solomon would have invested in during his time. Fortunately, we have some insight for today's financial climate. Robert Katz, (Katz, Robert. The Solomon Portfolio: How to Invest Like a King. Lake Mary, FL: DC Press, 2008. ISBN 978-1-932021-37-0) in his book, "The Solomon Portfolio" recommends the following 7 assets:

1. Large-cap U.S. stocks
2. Small-cap U.S. stocks
3. Non-U.S.stocks
4. Commodities
5. Real Estate Investment Trusts (REITs)
6. Intermediate bonds
7. Cash

Likewise, a Proverbs 31 investor would focus on broad-based diversification offering risk reduction using stocks, bonds, mutual funds, real estate, and other investment vehicles. Each of the asset classes will perform differently during different market conditions providing some level of protection from major losses in any one area.

DIVERSIFYING INVESTMENTS FOR LONG-TERM GROWTH

Diversification allows you to achieve a balance between growing your money and protecting it when things get tough by NOT putting all your eggs in one basket. Holding a diverse portfolio can capture part of the growth opportunity in different industries and geographic regions while providing income.

Additionally, you can line up your investments with your tolerance for risk and financial objectives. Conservative investors tend to apply Biblical sayings like, "Wealth gained hastily will dwindle, but whoever gathers little by little will increase it, Proverbs 13:11 (ESV). Investments that align with the conservative temperament would include more stable and fixed assets like bonds, dividend paying stocks, high yield saving accounts, money market funds, certificate of deposits, fixed annuities, Treasury securities, index funds, REITs. The other financial temperament would be a bold investor with an appetite for higher risk to achieve a greater and quicker return. Those who favor higher risk are comfortable with market fluctuations. They function at a level of informed boldness grounded in proven methodology. Their portfolio includes a mix of growth stocks, emerging market investments, technology, innovation funds, small cap stocks, cryptocurrency, venture capital, angel investing, leverage and inverse EFTs, Options Trading, real estate flipping, and commodities trading.

The Proverbs 31 woman is always aware of her household needs and the needs of her family; she also balanced her portfolio. She stays on top of her assets and rebalances the portfolio every year. Balancing helps maintain the right mix of investments for your risk tolerance and keeps your portfolio aligned with your investment strategy. If you diversify your investments to include a variety of instruments, your investment portfolio could be more balanced and positioned to withstand market downturns. When you choose this path, you are making your money work for you and the opportunity for increase abounds. Your financial goals are achievable.

LEVERAGING THE POWER OF COMPOUNDING

The idea of compounding, as it pertains to financial stewardship, represents a slow, steady, constant growth process. You earn on your earnings. The earnings are then reinvested which makes the base for the future returns progressively bigger. Imagine the Proverbs 31 woman using her returns to buy a field.

As time goes by, the power of compounding becomes more prominent. This reminds us to patiently embrace a long-term perspective. Investing early and holding allows any investments to experience the impact of time driven compounding and thus accumulate more wealth. This principle mirrors the Bible's teaching of steady growth instead of quick gain.

You will see the power of compounding over time. Thinking about your wealth accumulation as a steady progression accentuates the importance of patience. Investing early and holding positively exploits the impact of time driven compounding.

Consistent stewardship is demonstrated when we add to our investments, monitor the activity, and make timely adjustments. Rest in faith and watch compounding work on your behalf. Use the "Rule of 72" to imagine the growth possibilities at your fingertips. Assuming you are consistent, the rule of 72 states that if you divide 72 by your rate of return, you will determine how many years it will take for your money to double. For example, if your rate of return is 6%, dividing 72 by 6 yields 12. This means that it will take 12 years to double your investment.

Patience is definitely a plus because sometimes your investments will shrink instead of growing. When the economic conditions change, you will wrestle with an impulse to divest. Be careful how you react. Think your decisions through. Ask yourself, "Is this the time to buy more since everything is on sale?"

Leverage the power of compounding to increase the effectiveness of your strategy. How do you leverage the power of compounding? This can be done by allowing your investments to grow and by reinvesting your earnings over long periods of time. In the parable of the talents, the faithful servant took his money and put it to work with the exchanges and doubled his money. On the other hand, the unfaithful servant hid his in the ground (Matthew 25:14-30). Compounding is a timeless tool and principle that causes your money to grow while you sleep. That is a powerful testament to our financial stewardship.

FIVE-STEP GUIDE TO START COMPOUNDING

1 BEGIN EARLY

The power of compounding relies on time. Start early to give your investments more time to grow.Even small contributions can have a significant impact over the long term.

2 INVEST REGULARLY

Consistently contribute to your investment accounts. Whether it's a retirement fund, a brokerage account, or a savings plan, regular investments ensure a steady stream of contributions that can benefit from compounding.

3 REINVEST EARNINGS

Choose investments that offer dividends or interest payments, and reinvest these earnings back into the investment. By reinvesting, you add to the base principal, allowing compounding to work its magic on a larger amount.

4 CHOOSE TAX ADVANTAGED ACCOUNTS

Take advantage of tax-sheltered accounts like IRAs, 401(k)s, or other tax-advantaged plans. These accounts allow your investments to grow tax-free or tax-deferred, maximising the impact of compounding.

5 BE PATIENT

Compounding is not a quick-fix strategy. It requires patience and discipline. Stay committed to your investment plan and avoid making emotional decisions based on short-term market fluctuations.

LEVERAGING THE POWER OF COMPOUNDING

Take stock of your current investments. What types of assets do you currently hold, and how diversified is your portfolio? Write about any areas where you feel you could diversify further.

Reflect on the concept of diversification and its role in long-term investment growth. How can diversifying across different asset classes and industries help mitigate risk and maximize potential returns?

LEVERAGING THE POWER OF COMPOUNDING

Reflect on the concept of diversification and its role in long-term investment growth. How can diversifying across different asset classes and industries help mitigate risk and maximize potential returns?

LESSON SIX

UNLEASHING THE POWER OF PASSIVE INCOME

UNDERSTANDING PASSIVE INCOME AND ITS BENEFITS

Passive income is the time proven cheat code for financial freedom. Explore various passive income opportunities and diversify your income sources so that overtime, you will experience time independence, financial freedom, flexibility, and long-term prosperity.

Passive income reminds me of the Biblical principle of sowing and reaping. It refers to earnings generated with minimal active effort. Think of eating fruit or vegetables from plants that you seeded in the past. You had to put in the initial effort, but once that plant took root, you were able to enjoy its fruits with minimal effort. This approach provides returns even when you are not actively engaged in labor.

Sources of passive income include rental properties, dividends from investments, royalties from creative works, affiliate marketing, or online businesses. Each of these investment types, when implemented effectively, allow you to leverage time, your knowledge and skills, and your unique gifts, talents, and abilities.

Time, effort, and initial resources are needed to start the process. As your income streams grow and mature, they can gradually replace or supplement active income. This will provide financial security and independence. Moreover, passive income frees up your time so you can focus on other things outside of a job, or trading time for money. You can focus on your purpose and passion, spending quality time with family, or anything else that you are called to focus on. This flexibility is a reflection of the balanced life led by the Proverbs 31 woman, who manages her responsibilities while also caring for her household.

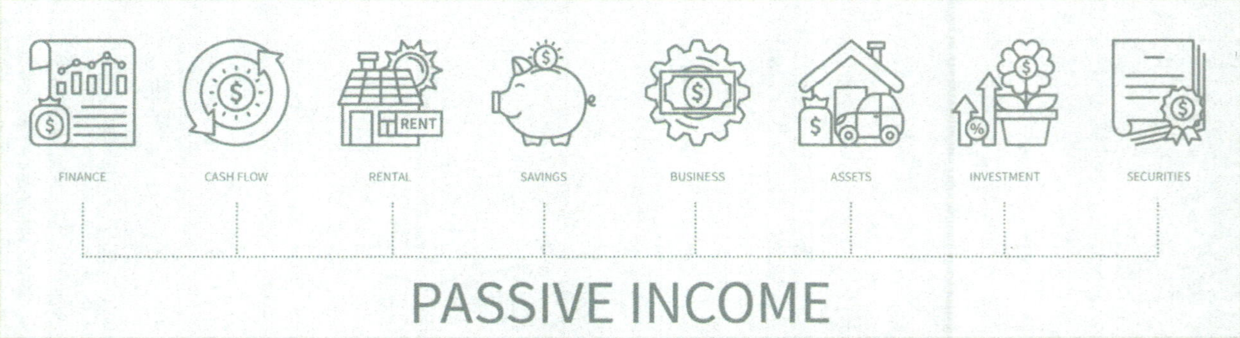

EXPLORING PASSIVE INCOME OPPORTUNITIES

Exploring specific passive income avenues like real estate, dividends, and royalties can present you with diverse options to build passive income streams.

Real Estate

Investing in rental properties or Real Estate Investment Trusts (REITs) embodies the Proverbs 31 principle of considering a field and buying it (Proverbs 31:16). These are a reliable way to receive passive income that will continuously come in, much like planting a seed and receiving a continuous harvest. Steps to take will include initial effort and perhaps capital, however, it will continuously produce rental payments or dividends.

Dividends from Stocks

Buy stocks from companies that pay dividend and become part owner. Because you are a part owner, you would receive a dividends payment from the company profit. Dividends are a good way to make passive income because it pays you part of the company profits on a regular basis which would supplement your regular income and contribute to financial growth.

Royalties from Creative Works

Creating intellectual property, such as books, music, or digital products, allows you to monetize your God-given talents and passions, earn consistently on work you've done once, and share your knowledge with others.

Research when you decide to implement these strategies. Connect with experts who can guide you and help you make good choices.

When you have real estate, stocks, and creative royalties, you not only increase your opportunities to generate passive income, you also spread your risk. When one investment instrument is down, you now have a more diversified and stronger passive income portfolio with some potential blow cushions, spread out to lessen being slammed by one thing.

Some would lead you to believe that building passive income happens overnight. Be patient because this type of investment will yield the greatest return over time. Know that when you work a sound strategy, rooted in wisdom, overtime you will reap the results of a secure financial future.

PASSIVE INCOME BRAINSTORM

What are some passive income ideas that align with your skills and interests?

What research can you do to find existing passive income opportunities to discover inspiration and potential avenues to pursue?

What financial goals do you want to achieve through passive income, and how can you align your pursuits with these goals?

What potential challenges or obstacles might you encounter while exploring passive income opportunities, how can you overcome them?

What specific steps can you take to actively explore and implement passive income streams?

PASSIVE INCOME BRAINSTORM

Use the space below to further brainstorm different passive income ideas which align with your interests and skills.

PASSIVE INCOME BRAINSTORM

LESSON SEVEN

FAITHFUL INVESTING:
A STRATEGY TO SEND YOUR MONEY TO WORK

UNDERSTANDING DIFFERENT INVESTMENT OPTIONS

1. Stocks

Stocks represent ownership in a company. Each share of stock you own equates to a percentage ownership of the company. You have a vested interest and legal claim to your share of the company's assets and earnings. Stock value fluctuates with the economy, the company's perceived performance, and other factors. Stocks offer the potential for high returns but also come with higher risks.

2. Bonds

Bonds are securities that are issued by corporations or governments to raise money, when you buy a bond you basically lend your money to the issuer in exchange of interest payments (coupon) made on a periodic basis and you get the principal amount back when your bond matures.

3. Mutual Funds

Mutual funds are pools of money from many investors and invest in a diversified portfolio of stocks, bonds and other securities. They are run by professional money managers and when you own shares in a mutual fund, you own a percentage of the cash in the collect portfolio, the diversify your investments across many assets. They are more appropriate for someone who wants to diversify their investments, but do not want to pick specific securities to trade.

4. Exchange-Traded Funds (ETFs)

ETFs are similar to mutual funds but can be bought and sold like individual stocks on a stock exchange. They can also offer diversified investing like mutual funds but give the flexibility trading like stocks during market hours. Cost is often lower than most mutual funds expense ratios.

5. Real Estate Investment Trusts (REITs)

REITs are companies that own or finance income-producing real estate. They also pay out at least 90% of their taxable income in the form of dividends to shareholders. They can help you diversify your income stream and take advantage of real estate's potential returns while investing in small and/or large chunks like stocks.

6. Certificate of Deposit (CD)

CDs are time deposits offered by banks with a fixed term and interest rate usually from three months to 5 years. These are very low risk investments compared to most others, so they also have a low return. The interest rate from a CD may vary depending on how long you "lend" money to the bank.

7. Commodities

Commodities are resources such as gold, silver, oil, or agricultural products, which are traded on exchanges around the world. A variety of factors influence the value of a commodity (supply and demand dynamics, geopolitical stability) and thus, the ultimate value of your investment(s).

8. Individual Retirement Accounts (IRAs)

IRAs (Individual Retirement Accounts) are tax advantaged accounts that allow you to invest in wide variety of investments including stocks, bonds, mutual funds, and ETFs. By using an IRA you can gain significant tax advantages which will help grow your retirement funds more quickly.

ASSESSING RISK TOLERANCE AND INVESTMENT STRATEGIES

The ability to take on risk is a vital part of investing. Generally, the more risk we are willing to take on, the greater the potential reward we will receive. There is a necessary balance here because high risk can yield high profit and loss. Understanding your risk tolerance is important because it helps determine the right mix of investments in your portfolio.

If you have a high-risk tolerance, you may be comfortable with more aggressive investments.
This could be useful for someone who wants to get as much return on their investment. If you on the other hand have a low risk tolerance, you may choose more conservative investments because you will still get your money back but have the potential to get lower to no returns.

Investors need to guard against frustration with investments by balancing their comfort levels with risk and complexity with their return requirements. Higher risk investments, such as stocks or equity funds, will generally yield higher returns than lower risk investments, such as certificates of deposit, savings accounts, or bonds. However, higher risk investments are also more likely to have significant short term declines in value. Furthermore, a young investor may need to endure some short term declines in value of their portfolios in order to have long term growth at the rate needed to meet their long term financial goals.

Diversification is a way to manage investments carefully by not putting all your eggs (money) in one basket. By spreading the investment across more asset classes and sectors, which will reduce the overall risk of loses to the total value of the investment.
Another crucial factor in determining the best investing strategy is the time horizon a person has until they need their money. If you have a longer time horizon, you can ride out the ebbs and flows of the stock market and take advantage of compounding returns.

ASSESSING RISK TOLERANCE AND INVESTMENT STRATEGIES

It is critical to re-assess your risk tolerance and investment strategies on a regular basis especially if you have a change in life circumstances, or are nearing retirement. Determining what your risk tolerances are, and then creating an investment plan to match those risk tolerances, is one of the key factors in creating a successful investment plan.

When deciding what investment strategies to use, you should consider working with a financial adviser. They can help you to accurately assess your risk tolerances and create an appropriate investment plan for you based on your needs and objectives. An adviser can also provide you with knowledgeable feedback on investing in the financial markets, guide you in making informed decisions according to your investment plans, and determine the level of risk that you are most comfortable with.

Investment strategies must begin with an assessments of your risk tolerance. This is arguably the most important part as your risk tolerance will help us create an investment plan that is right for you. Once you determine your risk tolerance, you will balance how much risk you can take on and how much return you are seeking. Your investment plan should be built based on your investment preference. In an effort to help bring your risk down and increase your protection, diversify your investment portfolio based on your goals and timeline.

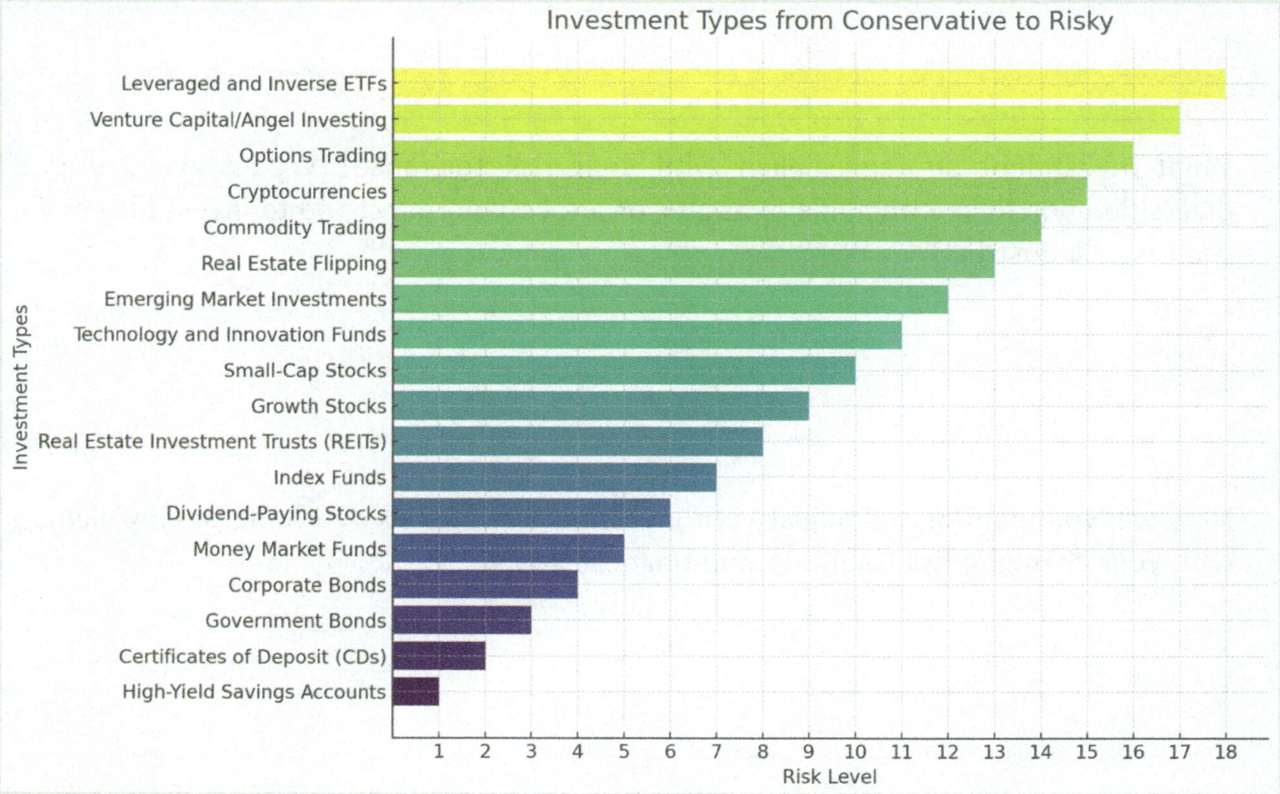

ASSESSING RISK TOLERANCE AND INVESTMENT STRATEGIES

What level of risk are you comfortable with when it comes to investing? Would you rather prioritise safety or pursue higher returns through potentially riskier investments?

How do your financial goals and time horizon influence your risk tolerance? Are you willing to take on more risk for long-term goals or prefer lower-risk options for short-term objectives?

Have you experienced investment losses in the past, and how did you react to them emotionally? How can you use these experiences to better understand your risk tolerance?

What investment strategies align with your risk tolerance? Would you prefer a diversified portfolio with a mix of assets, or are you more inclined to invest in specific sectors or industries?

How will you monitor and adjust your investment strategies over time to stay aligned with your changing risk tolerance and financial goals?

MAKING INFORMED INVESTMENT DECISIONS

Informed decisions are based on careful research, analysis, and consideration of various factors to mitigate risks and maximise returns. Understanding your financial goals, risk tolerance, and time horizon is the foundation of informed investing. Knowing what you aim to achieve and how much risk you are willing to take helps shape the appropriate investment strategy.

Conducting thorough research on different investment options, such as stocks, bonds, mutual funds, and real estate, is crucial. Each asset class has its unique risk and return characteristics, and understanding their dynamics helps in making appropriate investment choices.

Staying informed about market trends, economic indicators, and global events can aid in identifying potential investment opportunities and risks. Staying up-to-date allows you to make timely adjustments to your portfolio as needed.

Diversification is a key principle of informed investing. Spreading investments across various asset classes, industries, and geographic regions helps manage risk and reduce exposure to any single investment.

Seeking advice from financial advisers or professionals can provide valuable insights and expertise. Advisers can offer personalised guidance tailored to your unique financial situation and help you make informed choices.

Emotional discipline is vital in investment decision-making. Avoid making hasty decisions driven by fear or greed during market fluctuations. Staying focused on your long-term goals and maintaining a rational approach leads to more successful outcomes.

MAKING INFORMED INVESTMENT DECISIONS

MODULE 3

OVERCOMING CHALLENGES AND ALIGNING WITH CHRISTIAN VALUES

LESSON EIGHT

OVERCOMING ADVERSITY WITH FAITH AND FINANCIAL WISDOM

DEALING WITH FINANCIAL SETBACKS & UNEXPECTED EXPENSES

Establishing a Be of Good Cheer Emergency Fund

In the spirit of the Proverbs 31 woman, establishing an emergency fund is a wise strategy to prepare for unexpected expenses. This fund serves as a financial buffer, allowing you to cover essential needs during emergencies without resorting to credit or loans. It reflects the biblical principle of prudent preparation and stewardship.

Budgeting and Prioritization: A Balanced Scale

Creating a detailed budget is essential in managing financial challenges. This involves tracking your income and expenses to identify areas for cost-saving and prioritizing essential needs. This approach is in line with the biblical teachings of stewardship and wise resource management, ensuring that you make informed decisions in times of adversity.

Negotiate with Creditors: Seeking Graceful Solutions

If faced with financial hardship, reaching out to creditors can be a practical step. Many lenders offer hardship programs or flexible repayment options. This step can provide temporary relief and help navigate through financial challenges. When you deal with financial challenges, don't make the mistake of avoiding the problem. Reach out to your creditors and negotiate A reduced payment. Some lenders have hardship programs and flexible repayment options. This may not completely solve the problem, but it can reduce your stress.

Avoid New Consumer Debt at all Cost

Accumulating new debt that can add trouble to your trouble should be avoided. The Bible warns against the burdens of debt. Steer clear of high-interest loans or credit card debt to prevent added financial difficulties. We should adopt personal guidelines about what we will and will not use to purchase. For instance, consumer goods should be paid for outright or at least within the credit cycle because you don't want to owe on something that has already disappeared and not appreciated.

Seek Professional Advice: Wise Counsel Provides Safety

Consulting with a financial advisor or counselor reflects the biblical value of seeking wisdom in counsel. Professional guidance can help you analyze your financial situation from a Christian perspective and develop a plan to regain financial stability. This step is akin to seeking godly wisdom to navigate through life's challenges.

DEALING WITH FINANCIAL SETBACKS & UNEXPECTED EXPENSES

Trust God's Timing: Review and Adjust Financial Goals

Our goals are how we achieve our life vision. Sometimes we will adjust the timeline or nature of a goal based on the current financial environment. Don't beat yourself up but recognize that seasons come and go. Your situation will change multiple times over the course of your life. Plans and goals may change; However, God's plans for your life do not change.

A Faith Approach: Stay Positive and Focus on Solutions

The Proverbs 31 woman is described as laughing at the days to come, which reflects a sense of joy, hope, and positivity. It can be hard to maintain a positive mindset in the midst of financial setback. It is so important to reflect on God's promises and lean into what he says as opposed to what you see in the current moment. This mindset is a practice of faith and discipline where you focus on the word of God and what you can control. Work like it's all up to you and believe like it's all up to God. Seek support from your community of friends, family, and financial professionals. You are not alone so don't feel like you have to hide in your struggle.

Grow in Wisdom: Learn from Setbacks

Use financial setbacks as opportunities to grow in wisdom and understanding. Analyze what led to these challenges and take steps to prevent similar situations in the future, just as Proverbs teaches us to learn from experience and grow in understanding. Building resilience and financial literacy helps you navigate future challenges with greater ease and confidence.

Lean into Patience and Persistence

Recovering from financial setbacks requires patience and persistence, virtues extolled throughout scripture. Be patient with your progress and remain steadfast in your efforts to regain stability. Small, consistent steps, guided by faith and diligence, can lead to significant and meaningful progress over time.

BUILDING RESILIENCE IN THE FACE OF ECONOMIC FLUCTUATIONS

How have past economic downturns or fluctuations affected your financial situation and emotional well-being? What coping strategies did you employ during those times?

What steps can you take to diversify your sources of income to reduce vulnerability to economic fluctuations?

How can you build an emergency fund to provide a safety net during times of financial uncertainty? What amount would you consider sufficient for peace of mind?

Reflect on your current debt levels. How can you work towards reducing or managing debt to minimise its impact during economic downturns?

Research and explore investment options that historically demonstrated resilience during economic fluctuations. How can you incorporate these investments into your portfolio?

How can you improve your financial literacy and understanding of economic indicators to make informed decisions during uncertain times?

Consider the role of adaptability and flexibility in building resilience. What changes can you make in your lifestyle and spending habits to become more adaptable to economic shifts?

IDENTIFYING AND OVERCOMING SCARCITY THINKING

Learn from Financial Mistakes

Your financial mistakes do not define who you are, nor do they determine your intrinsic value. When you are recovering from financial setbacks, endeavor to learn from your past mistakes. Do better. Self reflect. Sit in God's presence and figure out the underlying issues that might have led to any poor decisions. This is a critical step to achieving financial growth and stability. Self reflection in the presence of God's will make his wisdom available to you. Acknowledge any past errors, prayerfully take corrective actions, and lay out a plan to make good decisions going forward..

Understand Financial Missteps

Identifying specific financial mistakes and analyzing their root causes is essential. This process of understanding what went wrong and developing effective solutions is akin to seeking discernment and knowledge, as encouraged in Proverbs. Gaining financial literacy is a vital component of this learning process, reflecting the biblical value of acquiring wisdom.

Set New Objectives and Seek Godly Counsel

Based on the lessons learned from past mistakes, setting new, realistic, and achievable financial objectives is key. This step mirrors the Proverbs 31 woman's strategic and intentional planning. Seeking professional advice can also provide valuable insights and tailored guidance, reflecting the biblical principle of seeking wisdom from others.

Craft a Resilient Financial Plan

A well-structured financial plan should focus on saving, investing, debt management, and contingency measures. Embracing resilience in the face of financial setbacks is crucial. Learning from past mistakes not only strengthens your ability to bounce back from challenges but also to adapt to changing circumstances, echoing the resilience demonstrated by many biblical figures.

Be Consist and Committed to your in Financial Growth

Consistency and dedication to new financial habits are essential. Financial growth takes time and patience, aligning with the scriptural encouragement to persevere and trust in God's timing. Be patient with the process, understanding that lasting change often requires time and steadfast commitment.

Celebrate Achievements with Gratitude

It is important to recognize and celebrate your achievements, no matter how small. This practice of gratitude is a biblical principle, reflecting a heart that acknowledges and appreciates God's provision and guidance in every step of financial growth and recovery.

IDENTIFYING AND OVERCOMING SCARCITY THINKING

What are some significant financial mistakes or decisions you've made in the past? What lessons can you draw from those experiences to avoid similar errors in the future?

How can you change your mindset about financial mistakes and view them as valuable learning opportunities rather than sources of regret?

Reflect on any patterns or recurring behaviours that may have contributed to your financial mistakes. What steps can you take to break these patterns and make more informed choices?

What potential challenges or obstacles might you encounter while exploring passive income opportunities, how can you overcome them?

What specific actions will you take to implement the lessons learned from your financial mistakes and create a more secure and prosperous financial future?

TRUE FULFILLMENT COMES FROM OVERCOMING CHALLENGES, NOT AVOIDING THEM.

LESSON NINE

ALIGNING MONEY WITH PURPOSE AND VALUES

EXPLORE THE CONNECTION BETWEEN MONEY AND PERSONAL VALUES

If you follow your money, you will be able to see your values, priorities, and beliefs. Your checkbook, how you spend your money is a reflection of these elements.

If you want to align your financial choices with your true aspirations so that you can lead a fulfilling life, get a handle on the connection between how you spend your money and your core values. This can be a very difficult inquiry because self-awareness and self introspection are sometimes difficult for us to achieve you have to make the decision you want to understand how your core values dictate your financial decisions or not.

For example, are you spending your money on charitable giving, and the vesting, or supporting causes that resonate with your desires. On the other hand, your financial decisions may not support these interests. Do you ever feel unsatisfied after making a purchase? When your spending is not in alignment, you can experience a sense of disconnection from your purpose.

To align your money with your values you will need to make conscious decisions where you intentionally allocate your financial resources to support what truly matters to you -- family, health, education, personal growth, or environmental sustainability. This alignment empowers individuals to lead purpose-driven financial lives. Your material possessions may provide comfort, but pursuing a purposeful life brings true contentment.

EXPLORING THE CONNECTION BETWEEN MONEY AND PERSONAL VALUES

What are your core personal values and beliefs? How do these values influence your attitudes and decisions regarding money?

Reflect on your spending habits and financial priorities. Do they align with your personal values? If not, how can you adjust your approach to money to better reflect what truly matters to you?

EXPLORING THE CONNECTION BETWEEN MONEY AND PERSONAL VALUES

Consider the impact of your financial choices on the world around you. How can you use your money in ways that align with your values and contribute positively to society and the environment?

How does your relationship with money affect your overall sense of fulfillment and well-being? Are there changes you can make to create a more harmonious connection between money and your personal values?

USE MONEY AS A TOOL TO SUPPORT YOUR ASPIRATIONS

Your spending should align with your values, as addressed before. We can be intentional about how we spend. When goals are set, attaching spending goals will positively reallocate your money for long term life gain. In this case the investment is your life and the direction you want it to go. How are you spending your money? Are you investing into personal growth, philanthropy, investing? The way we use our money should reflect our dreams.

Decide to be more disciplined in your spending. When you have a single positive experience with this new frame of mind, it will motivate you to keep going. It will become easier for you to aim your money at what aligns with your long-term life vision. Your choices encourage mindful consumption. This stops you from wasting money.

Financial planning is an opening to engineer a life that mirrors individual passions and ambitions. It consists of crafting a values-based budget, identifying long-term aspirations and constructing the road-map to live out them aspirations.

Living this way helps to bring us a sense of purpose and satisfaction. It takes the edge off of the drive to keep up with the Joneses and instead allows you to concentrate on personal growth and fulfillment.

To use money as a tool in the service of meaningful goals is to practice a kind of cash-consciousness that comes from understanding the deeper values of money—not only as it relates to your own well-being, but also to the well-being of the greater community, and the world as a whole. Philanthropy and the act of giving away ultimately become ways to make a difference, to put a dent in the world and to prove that you have the courage to show others what is possible.

If your ultimate goal is to lead a productive life on your own terms, ensure to earn money for what you want. As an end result, not only will you obtain possessions, but also bring your greatest passions to life.

USE MONEY AS A TOOL TO SUPPORT YOUR ASPIRATIONS

What are your most meaningful life goals and aspirations? How can money play a supportive role in achieving these objectives?

Reflect on the financial resources you currently have. Are they being utilized optimally to align with your meaningful goals? If not, what adjustments can you make?

Consider the potential trade-offs involved in using money to pursue your aspirations. What sacrifices, if any, are you willing to make to prioritise what truly matters to you?

How can you create a financial plan that allocates resources effectively to support your meaningful goals? What specific steps can you take to implement this plan and track your progress?

CREATING A PURPOSE-DRIVEN FINANCIAL PLAN

Identify Your Values & Aspirations

Consider what truly matters to you, such as family, health, personal growth, or contributing to a cause. Understanding your values will lay the foundation for a purpose-driven financial plan.

Set Meaningful Financial Goals

Based on your values and aspirations, set specific, measurable, achievable, relevant, and time-bound (SMART) financial goals.

Assess Your Financial Situation

Analyse your spending habits and identify areas where you can align your financial choices with your values.

Create a Values-Based Budget

Develop a budget that reflects your values and priorities. Allocate financial resources to support your meaningful goals and cut back on expenses that do not contribute to your aspirations.

Prioritise Debt Management

Address outstanding debts as part of your purpose-driven financial plan. Prioritise high-interest debts and work towards becoming debt-free, freeing up resources for pursuing your goals.

Build an Emergency Fund

Establish an emergency fund to cover three to six months' worth of living expenses. Having a financial safety net provides peace of mind during unexpected situations.

Invest with Purpose

Consider socially responsible investments or sustainable funds that reflect your ethical and environmental considerations.

Stay Committed and Flexible

Remain committed to your purpose-driven financial plan, but be open to adjustments as circumstances change. Life is dynamic, and your goals may evolve over time.

Seek Professional Advice

Consider seeking guidance from financial advisers who understand the importance of aligning money with values.

Review and Reassess Regularly

Regularly review your progress -celebrate milestones and be prepared to adapt to new opportunities and challenges.

What are your core values and beliefs in life? How can your financial goals be in harmony with these values?
Creating a Purpose-Driven Financial Plan

What are your long-term life aspirations and dreams? How can your financial plan support you in achieving these aspirations?

Consider any potential obstacles or challenges you may encounter along the way. How will you adapt your financial plan to overcome these hurdles and stay true to your purpose?

Reflect on your short-term and long-term financial goals. Are they purposeful and meaningful to you? If not, what adjustments can you make to align them with your values?

How can you use your money to positively impact others or contribute to causes that matter to you? What charitable or philanthropic goals do you want to incorporate into your financial plan?

Who can provide support or guidance as you work towards your purpose-driven financial plan? Are there mentors, financial advisers, or like-minded individuals you can seek advice from?

How will you measure progress and success in your purpose-driven financial plan? What milestones can you set to track your journey towards your meaningful goals?

How can you balance the pursuit of financial security and growth with the pursuit of a purposeful and fulfilling life? What trade-offs are you willing to make to stay true to your values?

Notes:

LESSON TEN

GENEROSITY AND GIVING: THE HEART OF THE PROVERBS 31 WOMAN

GIVING HAS A HUGE IMPACT ON YOUR PERSONAL FULFILMENT

Embrace a Generous Spirit

The Proverbs 31 Mindset includes generosity. Generosity includes the money we give; and it's also about the kindness we extend, the empathy we show, the volunteering we engage in. It's about love and serving other people, whether they deserve it or not. It's about the joy that comes by following God's example in loving and serving. It's about finding reward and fulfillment for the things you do and that resonates with the joy of living in God's will.

The Proverbs 31 woman reveals that "She opens her arms to the poor; yes, she extends her hands to the needy." (Proverbs 31:20, WEB). Her open-handedness is more than monetary. It includes acts of kindness, sensitivity, care, and involvement, which are all part of being and doing the love of Christ – again, that's our end purpose. A generous spirit engenders feelings of joy and deep fulfillment. "The liberal soul shall be made fat. He who waters shall be watered also himself." (Proverbs 11:25, WEB).

Align Giving with Values and Passions

Giving presents an opportunity to support causes and initiatives that are close to your heart, whether they are charities, environmental efforts, education, or social welfare. Your act of giving reflects your faith in action, your call to be a Christian and to care for other people and God's creation. Each act of generosity is a chance to make a difference, which could spread ripples of positive changes far beyond the benefit one would instantaneously see.

Giving benefits both the person who gives and the person who receives. These benefits also align with the Christian principle that it is more blessed to give that to receive (Acts 20:35). Giving improves personal well-being, enhances self-esteem, and strengthens social ties. It is a fitting social activity because so many of our current societal ills (stress, overwork, relational isolation, envy) – are, in fact, byproducts of individualism. We are social creatures and need to act like it.

GIVING HAS A HUGE IMPACT ON YOUR PERSONAL FULFILMENT

Be Intentionally Generous

Creating a giving strategy which is called "a giving plan" allows you to intentionally direct your resources to replicate your values, making a significant impact on the things in which you care about the most. This strategic act of generosity parallels the thoughtful and purposeful nature of the Proverbs 31 woman.

Volunteer

Using your time and abilities for others is a very useful way to be generous. Participating in community or volunteer work is a concrete way to help and support people who need it. Service to others is a key Christian principle. It demonstrates the Christian ideal of serving others and is a key way to show God's love in action. It makes God's love visible to people in practical ways.

Inspire Generosity in Others

What you choose to give and do for others inspires them to give and do for someone else. Generosity creates a chain reaction of kindness and touches people's hearts, encouraging a culture of compassion, empathy, and greater love. Quietly showing a concern for others is the recipe for a world more fully able to reflect the Christian vision of a community united in love and service.

GIVING HAS A HUGE IMPACT ON YOUR PERSONAL FULFILLMENT

What causes or issues are most important to you? Reflect on your passions and interests to identify areas where you would like to make a positive impact.

How can you incorporate giving back into your financial plan? What percentage of your income or assets are you willing to allocate to charitable giving or supporting causes that matter to you?

Consider the various ways you can give back beyond financial contributions. How can you volunteer your time, skills, or resources to support organizations or individuals in need?

Reflect on the potential benefits of giving back, not only for the recipients but also for yourself. How does generosity enhance your sense of fulfilment and well-being?

GIVING HAS A HUGE IMPACT ON YOUR PERSONAL FULFILMENT

What causes or issues are most important to you? Reflect on your passions and interests to identify areas where you would like to make a positive impact.

Reflect on the financial resources you currently have. Are they being utilised optimally to align with your meaningful goals? If not, what adjustments can you make?

Consider the potential trade-offs involved in using money to pursue your aspirations. What sacrifices, if any, are you willing to make to prioritize what truly matters to you?

How can you create a financial plan that allocates resources effectively to support your meaningful goals? What specific steps can you take to implement this plan and track your progress?

USING MONEY AS A TOOL TO SUPPORT MEANINGFUL GOALS AND ASPIRATIONS

Reflecting on Your Values and Aspirations with a Faith Perspective

Begin by turning inward and contemplating your heart's desires and ultimate goals in the context of your faith. What makes you happy and brings you a sense of meaning, and how does this relate to what you trust God is summoning you to do? Think about how your financial choices might advance these yearnings and objectives.

Creating a Budget Aligned with Your Aspirations

Dedicate resources toward the things you value, purposely pushing back and saying "no more" to things that don't matter and don't advance your cause. This process should reflect your commitment to the God-life, your commitment to living a life that honors Him and reflects who you are and what you are called to do.

Setting Clear, Specific Goals Aligned with Christian Values

Your Christian values and goals should form the basis of your financial goals. Set specific and measurable goals. Prioritize your goals and let them guide your financial decisions. A balanced goal should have the qualities of personal fulfillment and service to others as seen in the Proverbs 31 woman.

Celebrating Milestones as Acts of Thanksgiving

Recognize and rejoice in each milestone along your financial journey. Doing so strengthens positive financial behaviors, and it is an act of gratitude to God for His guidance and abundance. This practice encourages ongoing commitment and diligence in being a good steward of what you have.

Regular Review and Adjustment: Staying Adaptable in Faith

Review and evaluate your financial plan consistently, allowing for adjustments as God's will for your life becomes clearer or circumstances in life change. This flexibility is paramount so that your financial plan matches your variable goals and aspirations.

USING MONEY AS A TOOL TO SUPPORT MEANINGFUL GOALS AND ASPIRATIONS

Practicing Mindful Spending: A Conscious Decision

Take time to think before making purchases. The speed in which we can spend money without leaving the house is astounding. Perhaps, leave large purchases parked in your shopping cart for a few days to see if you still want it. Also, spend based on your life agenda and goals. At the beginning of your fiscal year, make a list of items you would like to purchase. Put them in priority order and plan for the purchase.

Practicing Gratitude: Strengthening the Connection with Aspirations

Nurture a grateful heart, knowing that every financial resource is a divine gift. Such an attitude will reinforce the link between your use of money and the realization of your heavenly visions and purposes.

Prioritizing Debt Repayment: A Step Towards Financial Freedom

One practice to consider is the establishment of a plan to become debt free. By crafting a plan to repay debts, especially high interest loans, you can free up resources to put to work toward your goals. By working to become debt free and avoiding the bondage of debt, you are better able to steward your finances. To get started, concentrate on discharging debts, particularly high-interest ones. As you become debt-free, you can allocate those resources toward your goals. Creating and executing a debt-removal plan is consistent with the biblical principle of refusing to live in debt bondage and instead pursuing financial stewardship.

Before buying anything, ask yourself how this outlay helps contribute to your goals. Stop and consider a purchase before completing it. Does the item or expense contribute to the goal God is leading you towards? Certainly, we can and should aspire to be contemplative in our giving and be purposeful in our saving and investing to the mutual joy of ourselves and God.

USE MONEY TO SUPPORT MEANINGFUL GOALS AND ASPIRATIONS

What are your most significant life goals and aspirations? How can you use your financial resources to support and bring these goals to fruition?

Reflect on the alignment between your financial decisions and your meaningful goals. Are your spending, saving, and investment choices in harmony with what truly matters to you?

Consider the trade-offs involved in using money to pursue your aspirations. What sacrifices, if any, are you willing to make to prioritize what is most important to you?

How can you create a financial plan that optimally allocates resources to support your meaningful goals? What specific steps can you take to implement this plan and measure your progress?

BALANCING GENEROSITY WITH FINANCIAL RESPONSIBILITY

Generosity is only responsible when we balance it with financial responsibility. You can give your resources in ways that do not accomplish your goals or to causes that do not really do the work they say they do. Generosity is most impactful when the causes agree with your vision, mission and goals. We all know that can include formal giving, helping family and love ones, and volunteering. Supporting loved ones can be a big issue. Sometimes, we need to step aside from helping family members who continuously make the same mistakes or are not trying to help themselves.

Financial responsibility is Biblical stewardship. You manage your money wisely: saving, sowing, and spending. This includes budgeting, saving, and investing. Learning how to manage your money so that you make solid decisions is a good example of financial responsibility. How you give to others must include boundaries so that you do not give more than is feasible. Balance is needed with friends and family. Balance is needed in your consumer spending. This balance sets the framework for your boundaries as a part of your stewardship.

Committing to giving as a part of your budget can help. Also, having a giving plan can make it easy for you to say no when necessary. This also helps you to give to the causes and passions that mean the most to you.

Review your financial plan regularly, this includes budgeting for annual, quarterly, and monthly expenses. Make adjustments along the way as your circumstances fluctuate.

Finally, do it all with a grateful heart.

LESSON ELEVEN

LIVING A LIFE OF FINANCIAL ABUNDANCE

ABUNDANCE IS PART OF EVERY AREA OF LIFE

1. **Abundance Mindset: See Through God's Eyes**

Cultivate a mindset that goes beyond just worrying about money. Understand that not only are there lots of opportunities for financial gain, but there are also plenty of chances for love and the kinds of experiences that make life truly worthwhile.

2. **Gratitude Practice: Recognize God's Blessings**

Be grateful for the things you already have. Recognize and cherish the people you call friends, the things you have achieved, the moments of joy you have experienced, and the personal growth you have made. Consider these your blessings from God.

3. **Positive Relationships: A Reflection of God's Love**

Work intentionally to maintain healthy relationships with your family, friends, and communities. You have so much to gain from these relationships – love, support, and the knowledge that you are not alone. You can't lose sight of what it means to be together, to have a communal life with others who share your values and goals.

4. **Personal Growth: Grow in Wisdom and Faith**

Strive to have an outlook that generates personal growth and self-improvement. Increase in wisdom and understanding. Make the most of the knowledge, skills, and the kind of growth potential that can give you a fuller, more joyous, and spirit-filled life.

5. **Time and Energy: Steward God's Gifts**

Your time and energy are valuable, limited resources. You should be very particular about how you use them. Cherish moments when you can make a difference in someone else's life, and seize opportunities that allow you to fulfill God's intentions.

6. **Creativity and Expression: Celebrate God-given Talents**

Develop your creative side. Let it blossom, enlarge, and enrich your life with expression. Appreciate the multitude of concepts, talents, and extraordinary gifts that you possess and can extend to better your world.

7. **Health and Well-being: Honor the Temple of God**

Put your physical and mental well-being first. See your body as the place where the Holy Spirit resides; treat it with honor and respect. Recognize that good health and healing are direct blessings from God.

8. **Abundance in Nature: Appreciate God's Creation**

Get in touch with the natural world. Experience the might and tranquility that it offers. Learn that nature is a representation of God—nature shows us what is known of God (Romans 1:19-20). The earth reflects the generosity of God by producing a great variety of environments that take care of us. He provided for us before we were created. Appreciate the power and peace He provides. Nature represents God. It offers beautiful landscapes to ease your anxiety and provide natural resources. The work of God's creative force is visible everywhere in nature. If you take the time to look, you have to be impressed by how generous God is to us.

INTEGRATING ABUNDANCE INTO ALL AREAS OF LIFE BEYOND MONEY

How can you cultivate abundance in areas such as relationships, health, personal growth, and fulfilment?

Reflect on areas of your life where you currently experience abundance. How can you replicate the mindset and actions that have led to abundance in these areas in other aspects of your life?

Consider any limiting beliefs or scarcity mindsets that might be holding you back in different areas of life. How can you shift your perspective to embrace abundance and open yourself up to new possibilities?

How can you express gratitude and practice abundance daily? What specific actions can you take to foster a mindset of abundance and attract more positivity into all areas of your life?

FINDING PEACE ON THE JOURNEY TO FINANCIAL ABUNDANCE

Embrace Growth and Self-Discovery

You will learn so much about yourself because money and wealth are personal. Your financial decisions are rooted in who you are. Commit to self reflection, growth, and kindness to yourself.

Celebrate Progress with Gratitude

It is easy to criticize your progress or to get impatient when you are not moving at an acceptable pace. Be patient and celebrate your wins every day. Give thanks to God because He has your back.

Align Your Actions with Your Values and Aspirations

Many people fail to achieve their financial goals because of misalignment. Take time to prioritize your values. Check your dreams and aspirations against your actions. If your actions do not match the dream, then change your actions.

Build Resilience in Challenges

Your challenges can be an opportunity to build faith and knowledge. Your experiences, positive and negative, build your resilience. Lean on God and watch Him give you the wisdom and guidance to make it to the next stage.

Develop A Positive Relationship with Money

Our view of money can be influenced by many factors. When we move from surviving to thriving by trusting God's provision, we let go of fear and scarcity thinking. Mindfulness is an activity that allows us to zoom in on how we feel about money. Financial decisions should not be thoughtful and intentional.

Nurture A Holistic View of Abundance

Understand that financial wealth constitutes more than just money. It also includes a sense of wellness that involves good physical and mental health and meaningful, close connections with others. Abundance allows room for personal growth and cannot be measured only in dollars.

INSPIRING OTHERS TO EMBRACE PROSPERITY AND FULFILL THEIR DREAMS

Leading by Example: Demonstrating Resilience and Faith

You have a great desire to leave a legacy and to impact people's lives for the better. The benefits of living a life that teaches can propel you to the life of your dreams. You start by expecting your intentional actions to yield personal results. Others see you and emulate you, which is great because this means that you are producing fruit in others. You are motivating others to move through obstacles and fear to seize the opportunities around them.

Sharing Knowledge and Expertise: A Form of Service

You can share what you know in at least two ways: paid and free. It is up to you to decide which is appropriate for various situations. You should get paid for what you know. On the other hand, service is a practice that pays generously also. Who will you mentor, teach, and train?

Celebrating Others' Achievements: Fostering a Supportive Environment

Collaboration over competition is the best way to live. When you adopt this mindset, it allows you to be comfortable celebrating the accomplishments of others. Create circles in which you and the others in your circle are encouraging of one another.

Encouraging Financial Literacy and Responsibility

Promote financial literacy and responsible money management to empower others to make informed decisions about their finances. Advocate wise financial habits and you will inspire them to build a solid foundation for their dreams.

Empathy and Understanding: Valuing Diversity in Prosperity

Think about other's circumstances as you build. Recognize their unique path and give support to help them achieve their aspirations. This is about compassion and empathy. Your efforts will be greatly rewarded.

Motivate Others to Grow and Change

Inspire others to fulfill their dreams by having a firm understanding of Biblical prosperity. You will see growth in yourself and your mentees. Lead by example to inspire others. Demonstrating resilience, determination, and a positive mindset in the face of challenges can inspire individuals to overcome their own obstacles and pursue their dreams. By promoting the idea that abilities and intelligence can be developed, you motivate others to embrace opportunities and strive for greatness.

INSPIRING OTHERS TO EMBRACE PROSPERITY AND FULFILL THEIR DREAMS

What are some personal experiences or stories of triumph over adversity that you can share to inspire others on their journey towards prosperity and fulfilling their dreams?

How can you actively support and encourage others in their pursuits? What specific actions can you take to lift them up and provide the motivation they need to overcome challenges?

Reflect on the lessons you've learned from your own path to prosperity. How can you install these lessons into actionable advice for others to apply to their own lives?

Consider the power of leading by example. How can you demonstrate a positive and purpose-driven mindset in your own life to inspire others to do the same?

LESSON TWELVE

CONCLUSION: NEXT STEPS

NEXT STEPS

The journey toward financial abundance has an enormous impact on your life. It powerfully shifts your mindset from seeing scarcity everywhere to seeing abundance instead. And think about that for a minute: What are we saying to God when we constantly tell ourselves and anyone who will listen that we don't have enough?

Once I stepped out of that worldview and started recognizing the abundance of what I already have in my life, my financial situation began to change. My foundation is solid; I've developed good money habits and see the many possibilities I have for creating income. If something happens, and it often does; I'm not thrilled about it, but I know I can bounce back because I have before.

People who live a life of financial abundance understand that adversity is just a part of life. They know that when life gives you lemons, you don't just make lemonade with it – you figure out how to leverage the lemonade to create abundance.

FINAL THOUGHTS

The goal of this workbook is to motivate you to think differently about abundance. A Christian woman should expect an increase or yield from her work. You should be paid well for the work you perform. The truth of the matter is that women are often paid a significantly smaller salary than men. The pay gap is real! Women also spend their income on family and community at a significantly higher amount than men. This sometimes prevents us from saving and taking proper care of ourselves.

I chose to cement this discussion with the Proverbs 31 woman. I wanted you to have a Biblical vision of a woman who cares for her home through multiple channels. She is a homemaker, an entrepreneur, and a community activist. She is willing to work, make investments, and has income to make purchases.

My hope is that this workbook motivates you to change any habits that you need to change. Don't judge or feel guilty about your current situation. Move forward intentionally. Be gentle with yourself. Take time for you! Set aside financial resources for yourself.

Made in United States
Orlando, FL
05 November 2026

90207824R00072